YOUR KNOWLEDGE HAS VALUE

Bibliographic information published by the German National Library:

The German National Library lists this publication in the National Bibliography; detailed bibliographic data are available on the Internet at http://dnb.dnb.de .

Imprint:

Copyright © 1998 GRIN Verlag, Open Publishing GmbH
Print and binding: Books on Demand GmbH, Norderstedt Germany
ISBN: 9783668557826

This book at GRIN:

http://www.grin.com/en/e-book/378232/advertising-and-advertising-as-a-type-of-discourse

Angelika Felser

Advertising and Advertising as a type of discourse

GRIN Publishing

GRIN - Your knowledge has value

Since its foundation in 1998, GRIN has specialized in publishing academic texts by students, college teachers and other academics as e-book and printed book. The website www.grin.com is an ideal platform for presenting term papers, final papers, scientific essays, dissertations and specialist books.

Visit us on the internet:

http://www.grin.com/

http://www.facebook.com/grincom

http://www.twitter.com/grin_com

Advertising and advertising as a type of discourse

Guy Cook: Ads as a type of discourse

Cook considers advertisements to be a type of discourse. A discourse analysis consists both of an analysis of language and an analysis of the context of communication.

The reason for this is that there is no act of communication without participants, intertext, situation, paralanguage, etc.

Advertising is not static, but a dynamic synthesis of many components. Acccording to Cook, one has to take into account

- the co-text (text which precedes or follows the text under analysis)
- the function
- music and pictures
- the paralanguage (the behaviour accompanying language such as facial expressions, gestures, the voice quality)
- participants (are part of the context and observers)

are senders - addressers - adressees - receivers

the advertising agency: sender - actor: addressor

the adressee: might be a specific target group

the receiver: anyone who sees the ad

the receiver is not always the adressee (for ex. a man watching a tampon ad)

- situation (relation of objects and people)
- the substance/material.

Generally speaking, there are a lot of different discourse types such as consultations, conversations, jokes, lessons, plays, prayers, stories, etc.

Since there are different ways of categorising these discourse types (by function, participants, situation substance, etc.), the discourse types can merge into each other. That is, a discourse can be several types at once.

Characteristic features of an advertisement

- ads seek to alter adressees' behaviour

- ads are contrained by the need to fulfill the wishes of their clients

- ads foreground connotational and metaphorical meaning and make use of paralanguage

- ads are embedded in accompanying discourses and are, therefore, parasitic [they often occur in the middle of a TV broadcast together with other ads]

- ads in their use of language are multi-submodal and can use writing, speech, song either singly or in combination as the medium permits:

within the language of TV ads there is a preference for the sub-modes of song and speach over writing, as music and song are able to create specific connotations such as cheerfulness or gloominess

[for example: music accompanies ads for ice cream to evoke cheerfulness and summer]

- ads constantly change and have the typical restless instability of a new discourse type

Advertisings as a type of discourse

First of all, it is wrong to say that advertizing differs from other types of discourse by its selling function, given that its aim is to persuade people to buy a particular product.

There are ads which don't sell anything; their functions are to amuse, to inform, to warn or to worry:

Exaples: „Your best friend is the one who won´t buy you a drink when you are driving"

In a German ad advertisers showed a child´s face with sad eyes and a sign covering his mouth saying „closed because of loneliness":

Just like all types of discourse, ads can overlap with other types of discourse types, such as conversation, films, political propaganda, songs, etc.

Ads are very often not valued as highly as other discourse types, such as journalism, law or science. They may be described in terms of their social function, but it is interesting to see that societies may be categorized in terms of the types of discourse they use and in terms of the way they use these types of discourse: Ads can reflect differences between cultures and different values, for instance,

In a Japanese ad for a marriage agency a woman says „As I would like to have

a bright child, maybe I could meet a graduate of Tokyo University".

However, it is important to see that the ad mirrors a different but by no means any inferior way of thinking, and that and that ads can also indicate social changes:

> Ads were quite rare in Eastern Europe under communism. Their absence particularly struck visitors from capitalist countries - and the other way round: Visitors to the West were overwhelmed by the quantity of ads in daily life, for example, in newspapers or on walls of metro stations.

Ads also have the power to change society. It depends on our attitude towards ads, our personality, our social and ideological position if and to what extent we are influenced by ads.

Adverts often appeal to ambition, greed and worry. Many of us urge to consume more and more because ads might make us feel dissatisfied or inadequate:

> Ads can make you feel unsatisfied, as before you watched a particular ad on television, you haven´t even had the slightest idea that you were lonely.
> "Fortunately", there are alcoholic drinks, and on TV, people having such a drink never seem to be alone. They are always involved in society, that is, surrounded by good friends. Paradoxically, in reality, alcoholic drinks consumed in excess make you lonely, as you are avoided by society
> "Fortunately" the lack you now realize is liquidated by the product.
> Thus, ads have got two functions: The articulation of fear and lack (failure, loneliness) and the liquidation of the lack articulated before.

Guy Cook: The World of an ad

The world of the sender is to manifacture the product.

The fictional world of characters are secondary participants on a TV commercial or in a newspaper ad. This, however, is the phantasy world of the addressee whereas his real world is the place where to buy the product.

Thus, the aim of the advertiser is to introduce the product into the audience's worlds via their phantasy or dream world. The product is the bridge between d of the ad and the reality of the adressee.

According to Torben Vestergaard and Kim Schroder adverts function on the level of a day-dream, as they make use of our desire for identity and a better world. The ultimate desire of advertisers is to make athe consumer to attach the desired identity to a particular product and, thus, to transform the need for identity into a need for commodity.

This is called "the added value" of a product, since the product can give you more.

They also claim that the product is no mass product:

In an advert for the coffee "Dalmeyer Prodomo" , for example, a woman adjusts apron-strings while enjoying her coffee.

In the advert for the beer "Roling Pilsener", the advertisers ad the slogan "als wärs für Sie allein gebraut" ("As if it has been brewed only for you") . By addressing the consumer directly, the advertising slogan is intended to make the customer believe that the product has been produced for the individual customer only. This is called the "You-Pathos", a direct appeal to the consumer suggesting individuality.

Another important fact is that advertisers adapt their ads to the context of culture („Zeitgeist"). As a result of a changing society, ads change in turn – like a circle.

Guy Cook: Categories of ads

According to Cook, the consumer, a short or long copy, the frequency, the medium, the product and the technique used can serve as parameters to categorize ads.

He points out that printed ads are static and enable us a closer observation of the text [exceptions: ads on subway trains and platforms which are longer copies]

Spoken ads, like TV commercials are non-static. The spoken and written text disappears quickly, so that the emotions being evoked remain elusive.In these texts a large variety of modes are offered at once (music, pictures, print, speech), and the interpretation of the text can be manipulated.

Cook differenciates between different **techniques** for different products.

Thus, he differenciates between product ads and non-product ads.

Within product ads, he makes the distinction between luxuries (chocolate, holidays, perfume) and necessities (cars, household: eggs, fridges, soap, etc.).

Non-product ads are, for example, ads for charities or political parties.

The choice of technique clearly relates to the product, the medium and the copy lenghts.

A "reason ad" is more useful in a long copy, for exaple in a magazine. It wouldn't work on a 30 second TV commercial. A reason ad is often used for expensive items which merit a long consideration (for example a car).

The "reason ad" makes a practical appeal:

a washing liquid is better than all the others as is washes more dishes and is more economic than any other product.

In contrast to the "reason ad", the "tickle ad" makes an appeal to emotion and mood:

Marlborough ad: „Come to Marlborough county". It promises adventure and total freedom.

As far as "short copies" and "long copies" are concerned, one can categorise ads also according to the consumer or better the "Target group": "Tickle ads" may work better on younger people than older people (see the various ads concerning the Anti-Aids campaigns or ads for products generally bought by women, for example sanatary towels. "Jewellery" is probably rather bought by the richer part of the population than by young people.

Cook also differenciates the so-called "hard sell" from "soft sell".
In a "hard sell-ad" a person makes a direct appeal to the audience.

For example, a man in a suit standing in front of a pile of carpets talks loudly and directly to the camera about cost, availability and guaranteed reliability]

In a "soft sell-ad" the audience is given a reason without any direct appeal. It rather relies on the mood than on exhortation. It implies that life will be better with this product, and contains un unspoken premise.

For instance, the Visa Card seems to make life so easy and convenient, so that you've always money wherever you go - even if you go swimming.

Another technique frequently used has to do with the frequency of ads release.
Cook differenciates between "slow drip" and "sudden burst".
Advertisers make use of "slow drip" when products are to be offered that are not dependent on seasonal variation. These products suggest reliability and durability (for example cars).
The technique of "sudden burst" is used to scamble wildly for attention, for instance before Easter or Christmas.Before Easter the industry offers chocolate in particular shapes, such as in forms of hares or eggs.
Before Christmas, not only chocolate is produced in various shapes, but also toys. These products diminish in January.

Renate Lachmann: Model of Textbildung

According to Renate Lachmann, the "Model of Textbildung" consists of 3 operations:

1) "inventio" - being the thematic operation
2) "dispositio" - being the operation of building up sequences
3) "elocutio" - being the operation of linguistic formulation of the text

The copywriter has to consider the context and , thus, choose between several opportunities

Jacques Dubois and his "groupe µ" at the Centre d´Etude poétique at the university of Liège aimed at creating a "Rhétorique générale". This was supposed to be applicable to narrative forms (comic, drama, novel, strip), lyrics and non-verbal, visual forms (advertising, film, photographie, sculpture, etc.).

The members of Dubois' group worked on the third component of "Textbildung", the "elocutio" and looked at the structure of language:
They structured it into different levels (grammatical, graphological, morphological, phonological, semantic and syntactic) by means of classification and segmentation.
The result is an inventory consisting of phonemes, morphemes, sememes, etc.

To these different levels of language, they applied the **"rhetorical operations"** of

- "adiectio" (addition) – to add an element

- "detractio" (deletion, substraction) – to leave out an element ["He done, I lay back down in the tub"]

- "immutatio" (substitution) - to put an element where another element should be

- "transmutatio" (permutation) – to put an element where it does not belong ("O Miserable nation - "O nation miserable")

They took the level "**Zero**", the neutral form of expression, into particular account. They have called it the "**Zero structure**".
According to Dubois and his group, "Isotopy" is the pleasure of recognition, the "unexpected regularity".

In contrast to "Isotopy", **Metaboly** means the pleasure of surprise, the unexpected irregularity".
A pattern broken by any unpredictable element, any change of any aspect of the language, any divergence from the neutral situation evokes "the feeling of adventure or jamais vu"
(John Livingston Lowes) .
Metabolies are deviations from the (text)norm or the social context.
They make the language stick out and, thus, they make the reader become aware of language.

Examples: All letters are written in small letters, but one letter is different.
     We know quite well that a cow is generally brown or black in colur - not purple (the
     MILKA-cow) or that bowls are not as big as the Asee-kugeln in Münster, Germany.

Despite the absence of any definition of norm and deviation, there is a substantial agreement among speakers about instances of both.

Examples for deviation:
The neutral forms of „He was pleased" or „It was freezing" are transformed by means of the "addition" of elements on the morphological level and "permutation" on the syntactical level into "Jesus, was he pleased" and "God, was it freezing".

These deviations can occur on any level:

Metagraphs are deviations on the graphological level:
Germany : Cigaretten; Great Britain: Kodak (substitution, "immutatio")

Metaphones are deviations on the phonological level:
("´tis" instead of "it is" is an aphesis)

Metamorphs   free and bound pre-or suffixes combined with morphemes are deviations on the morphological level.

Metataxe is a deviation on the syntactical level:

Examples:
"Toys us" (normal syntactic sequence: "We are Toys")
Other characteristics are "allographs" (coloured letters, three dimensional letters, a reversed R [which alludes to children beginning writing])
In the English language, "Night and Day" evokes the feeling of exoticism

"Allographs" (the colour of type, the form of type and the manner of type are good mind stickers:

Examples: the o in "Tschibo", "Centro" or in "Kool Milds"

Another example is when the colour in the text suddenly changes, for instance, from black (norm of the text) to red or blue.

Also, a sudden change of the manner of type, like the change from "antiqua" to "fracture", etc. makes us aware of language.

Allographs (small letters versus capital letters) and change of type size occur often together:

These, refer, of course, to special effects, such as congruity, elegance, emphasis and affectation.

Jacques Dubois and his "groupe μ" only consider figures of selection (deviations) which have been produced on the paradigmatic level. They consider rhetorical figures, such as "assonance", "alliteration" and "rhyme" to be results of "addition". Maybe, these are more likely to be figures of equivalence.

According to Guy Cook and Greg Myers, "**Isotopies**" are any recurrences of equal or similar elements. They fulfill our expectations and evoke a pleasure of recognition, a feeling of déjà vu: The receiver feels familiar with the product. Isotopies and paralellism are necessary for the coherence of a text.

Just like "Metabolies", Isotopies can occur on any level and are called according to the respective level:

Isographs

Isophones   ("I fly bleifrei"; "I like Leika": (assonance: rhyming of vowels; alliteration: repetition of consonants especially at the beginning of a word))

Isomorphs

Isotaxes

Isosemem: also refers to colours (chromems), types

rhyme: "A toast to the host"

repetition of voiceless sounds: "You take picture after picture after picture, because we have perfected pentax after pentax after pentax"

metaphor : a comparison without "like" or "as" , for example a girl is a rose

simile: a comparison with "like" or "as", for example "a girl like a rose"

personification

synechdoche : (pars-pro-toto): a part signifies the whole, for example „by sail" for „by ship"

added value "more than a..."

difference topos, for example "There is nothing quite like Mac Donald´s"

Deviations and figures of equivalence can occur at the same time and, thus, provoke pleasure of surprise and pleasure of recognition at the same time:

Example: "Put a tiger in your tank" is a semantic anomaly or metaboly, because the Tiger is standing for Powerful Petrol; in addition, there is phonic equivalence or isotopy: tiger – tank.

In the domain of **icons**, the transformation of the extra-linguistic world is of particular importance, as this creates rhetorical figures.

Icons are motivated as they have a relation of similarity to signifié: On photos, a bottle of perfume in an ad is an icon. The relation of "signifiant" and "signifié" is 1:1.

Symbols have got an arbitrary relation to the signifié. The colour red is a symbol for "love"

Icons and Symbols are marked by convention.

Metaphors are combinations of two synechdoches, a generalizing one and a particularizing one:

The German word "Drahtesel" is a metaphor for a "bike".

By "detractio", the deletion of semes (the generalizing synekdoche), the speaker realizes the common feature, means of locomotion. By "adjectio", the addition of semes (the particularizing synechdoche), the German speaker realizes a donkey.

Symptoms and indexes are marked by determination:

The index has a relation of contiguity to the signifié ("smoke" for "fire", "dialect" for "regional origin")

Symptoms have a causal relation, that is "cough" stands for "a cold".

Dubois and his group distinguish between "heterogeneous transformation" and "homogeneous transformation" in this context :

A "heterogenious transformation" is a kind if "substitution" or "immutatio": Only one element has been changed while all about stay as they were, for example

- with the "Milka cow" the normal colour has been deleted and the purple colour has been added
- in a black-and-white ad only the product is presented as colourful (perfume)
- in ads for detergents, for example, the product is presented as proportionally bigger than its environment. To suggest its mildness, the product has got a less high degree of saturation than its environment.

A "homogenious transformation" is some kind of "deletion", as all elements have been changed. This is with all black and white ads, for example.

Geoffrey N. Leech: AIDA-formular

A= to **attract** the reader's or viewer's **Attention** by something surprising or unexpected departing from the conventions (or rules of language)

I= to **arouse Interest** in the product

D= to **create Desire** to buy the product; to show the "unique selling proposition" of the product that makes it different from all the other products

A= to **make Action easy**; linguistically by means of a hyperbolic and exaggerated language (superlatives, claim of uniquenes) and imperatives, sometimes by means of samples and vochures initiating the consumer to go and to buy the production immediately

Register

According to Leech, registers are varieties of the English language distinguished by use in relation to the social context. The language of advertising which is different from other English registers is such a register. Halliday, one of the linguists of the London School of linguistics, contributed greatly to the formation of the term "register". According to him, varieties depend on semantical and, consequently, on grammatical, lexical and phonological choices.

In contrast to Halliday, Leech considers lexical differences of register to be more important than grammatical ones. According to him, register is related to the linguistic performance, not to the speaker 's linguistic competence:

- Register is a variety according to use – wheres a dialect is a variety according to the user
- Register is a particular selection of words and structures according to what one is doing at the moment
- A dialect is a specific kind of register which is related to a specific group of speakers according to their age, gender, regional origin and social status or and which derives as phonological, lexical, grammatical differences (variety according to the user)
- The language of advertising makes use of other registers to evoke the pleasure of surprise or recognition. Thus, advertisers borrow words from different registers, such as fairy tales, novel, poetry, scientific language, etc. This is what Leech calls "role borrowing", the "Chameleon technique" or "switching in registers".
- Like any other register the advertising register is relative, not absolute.
- People are often unaware of the register with which they operate
- A register is statistically measured by means of the three dimensions medium, role and style of discourse

Geoffrey N. Leens points out the particularities of the register of advertising as follows:

He emphasizes the particular advertising situation:

In a TV commercial, for instance, the participants are the advertisers (first persons) and the consumers (second persons). The relevant object is the product. The medium is speech, writing and TV. The purpose is to promote sales of the product to the consumer.

The audiences are different types of consumers. Therefore, the advertisers consider different codes, an eleborate code or a restricted code of language. We can often find a formal language in ads and commercials for medecin ($\rightarrow$ information, objectivity) and slang in ads and commercials for young people. Thus, the choice of language depends on the product and the consumer. Nouns are concrete and refer directly to product, adjectives can be highly´informative. In ads and commercials for women´s clothes, there are often adjectives such as "soft", "warm", "practical" and "washable".

The advertisers can communicate with the consumers either by means of direct address or by means of indirect address. Here they make use of a secondary participant.

In the situation of direct address, the first person (advertiser) and second person (consumer) are primary participants, being in a primary situation. Monologue and dialogue can also occur in direct address.

On TV, direct address is often realized by "supers", printed messages on the screen, or by commentaries, "voice over".

 The language used can be quite homogeneous, informal, colloquial and personal. Imperatives are typically used. The „I" or „we" are often avoided. The language is often that of a pure salesman, using short slogans, brand names, price labels. Commentaries are to draw attention to what happens on the screen. Words such as „here, now, this", imperatives „look, see, watch," the 2nd person pronoun "You" are often used. Brand names are repeated, adjectival compounds, demonstrative pronouns like „this, these", comparatives such as „better, healthier" and superlatives „the best, the finest" can often be found.

In an indirect (secondary) address situation, a secondary participant addresses the consumer either in form of a monologue or in form of a dialogue.

In the monologue, the secondary participant addresses the consumer direct, for example "„I use x all the time" (soap "CD"). A monologue can occur in form of a soliloquy. In this case the recipient is not addressed. In a dialogue or polylogue, the secondary participants enter in discourse with one another. The 3rd person secondary participants are people who occur in an ad and who are talked about (but who do not say anything, like the Milka cow).

On TV, the participants return to the primary situation at the end of the commercial, especially following a dialogue.

The aim of the **secondary** participant is to hold up a mirror to the consumer. He represents a portrait of the average member of the consumer public, a person, the average viewer is to identify with.[1]

Secondary participants can be:

- celebrities ($\rightarrow$ increase credibility of the product)
- satisfied customers
- apparent neutral persons
- ordinary housewifes, housemen ($\rightarrow$ identification)
- people caught in the act of using the product
- people involved in the production of the article ("Dr. Best")

Particular types of secondary participants:

- animals (Milka cow; the esso tiger")
- cartoons (HB Männchen)
- the idol (Marlboro man; $\rightarrow$ imitation)
- deus ex machina (classical drama, sudden appearance - being lifted up; here: a person appears to prevent a "catastrophy" in everyday life, for example "Klementine")
- a teacher (("Mr. Persil", "Tilly" (Palmolive"), Thomas Gottschalk (wine gum); $\rightarrow$ objectivity)

By using recurrent figures, the consumer associates the figures with the brandname.

---

1 Vgl. ggf. Jerzy Kosinski, <u>Being There</u> (Black Swan) and his interview with David Sohn „A Nation of Videots":
1993d. "A Nation of Videots." Interview by David Sohn. In Conversations with Jerzy Kosinski, ed. Tom Teicholz. Jackson:
University of Mississippi Press

Classification of the social context of advertisements according to the three levels style/tenor of discourse, mode of discourse and role of discourse to predict semantic peculiarities of the register advertisement:

- **style / tenor of discourse**

What is the relation between the partners of communication like?

the colloquial style (rather than formal style) is used

$\rightarrow$ one can get in contact with the general public more easily;

typical: the use of phrasal verbs ("find out", "fill in")

the casual style (rather than ceremonial (polite)) is used

$\rightarrow$ friendly, personal communication, typical: means of prosiopesis - initial elements have

zero exponents ("Found it?" instead of „Have you found it?")

the personal and impersonal style is used

$\rightarrow$ personal: 1st and 2nd person, exclamations, imperatives

$\rightarrow$ impersonal: 3rd person, passive voice - associated with anonymity

$\rightarrow$ advertisement: „You must get it" , „we are the best"; pasive voice "This is made from..."

- **mode of discourse**

How is the message transmitted? (spoken - written - written to be spoken (scripted)?)

A written message is more formal; a spoken message is more colloquial and makes use of many repetitions

Advertising English often resembles the restricted language of catalogues or road-signs ("No entry" (abbreviated grammar).

- **role of discourse**

What role does advertisement play in society?

Is it one of the public roles of language (like journalism, literature)?

Usually public roles do not use much linguistic specialization (for example the language of law), but the register of advertisement seems to comprise both a standard advertisement English which tends towards conformity with linguistic conventions and a non-conformity language with deviations (neologisms) to attract attention.

Standard components of press advertisements (Copy-sections):

The headline

The headline is together with the signature line one of the most indispensable parts; it is rarely omitted. It is a « ligne d' accrochage », an eye-catcher. It depends on the headline if a consumer becomes interested in the product or not. It is to draw attention (A - IDA) to itself. Often a picture draws attention to itself first. The headline is to make the consumer read the copy. Often, the advertisers articulate a lack (fear) and liquidates the articulated lack in the following body copy. Often, they make use of a parasitic structure ("All man are created ..."). Statements cause questions which could be answered by following body copy.

Deviations are used to create pleasure of surprise. They make use of particularities concerning typography (rarely used letters, allographs, neologisms) and make use of homophones.

Pleasure of recognition is created by equivalent elements and phonological rhetoric figures, such as alliteration, assonance, rhyme and parallelism.

Pictures

Pictures are optional, but are usually put. Pictures are often a very good eye-catcher and attract the consumers' attention.

The Body Copy

The body copy is often the main part of the ad's message. It is often devided into various sections under subheads and links the headline and the signature line. Its function is to arouse interest in the product and to create desire to buy this unique product (A- ID- A): Thus, it gives all the information an ordinary consumer might want to ask and liquidates the articulated lack. In addition, it informs about the unique selling proposition and proposes added value:

For example, a particular cream does not only prevent from wrinkels, but also gives you beauty, youth, happiness, love. According to Myers: "The trick is to be different like other people". Due to the "principal of positiveness", advertisers avoid words, such as "not", "never", "no").

Signature line

The signature line is the most important part as it contains the product's slogan. The brandname is, again, embedded in the slogan. The logo is the visualized realization of the brandname. The function of the slogan is that of a mind-sticker. It is to make the consumer familiar with the product and its brandname.

Standing details are optional, can provide useful information in small print, such as the address of the firm, its telephone number or homepage address on the world-wide-web.

Bibliography and guide to further reading:

Bergmann, Rolf, Pauly, Peter, Schlaefer, Michael (1981), Einführung in die deutsche Sprachwissenschaft, Carl Winter Universitätsverlag, Heidelberg.

Cook, Guy (1992), The Discourse of Advertising, London, New York.

Groupe μ (1977), Rhétorique de la poésie: lecture linéaire, lecture tabulaire.

Kosinski, Jerzy (1983), Being There, Black Swan.

"A Nation of Videots." (1993) Interview by David Sohn. In Conversations with Jerzy Kosinski, ed. Tom Teicholz. Jackson: University of Mississippi Press .

Leech, Geoffrey N. (1966), English in Advertising: a linguistic study of advertising in Great Britain, London.

Myers, Greg (1994), Words in Ads, London, New York, Sydney.

Ostheeren, Klaus, „Konzepte strukturalistischer und generativistischer Rhetorik", in: Zeitschrift für Literaturwissenschaft und Linguistik, 43/44, S. 133-143.

Vestergaard, Torben, Kim Schroder (1985), The language of advertising, Basil Blackwell.

YOUR KNOWLEDGE HAS VALUE